AF406284

Timeless KNOWLEDGE

AHBRIEA BROWN

Copyright 2026 by Ahbriea Brown

First Printing, 2026
Published by: Williams Commerce
ISBN: 979-8-9950472-6-1

Author

IG | X | YouTube: @ahbriea

Publisher

Williams Commerce, LLC
IG | X | Facebook: @wcwriting1
Visit Our Website: Williamscommerce1.com

Table of Contents

Introduction

Most people feel like they aren't capable of hearing from God. Some may even question if God is even listening to them or can hear them. Some people feel like answers can only come from church, but what happens when you go to church and still don't hear or feel anything?

Do you start to feel like only certain people or "God's favorites" can hear from Him? Do you start to question if you've done too many bad things, or have too many bad habits that are stopping you from communicating with Him?

The reality is that God is within us, not in the sky, not in a church, or in the Bible. He dwells inside us, so the closer we get to Him intimately, the better we recognize His voice. We have to stop putting God in a box and limiting Him by imposing predetermined ideas about how He should or can talk to us.

Once you realize and believe that God dwells within you, you will realize He knows all your thoughts and moves before you make them. Do you want to start or strengthen an intimate, sacred relationship with God that only you and Him understand (because, let's be honest, when it comes to the relationship, nobody else should matter)?

Start by disregarding every rule and stipulation society has put in your head about how a relationship with God is "supposed" to look. Shaping your relationship with God based on society's standards or traditional religion is detrimental and will keep you stagnant.

A relationship with God is supposed to run deeper than a routine and practices. Can those things aid you? Absolutely, but the foundation of a relationship with God should be based on intimacy. If you're intimate with God first, instead of being traditional first, no one can ever lead you astray because you know Him for yourself first.

However, learning practices and traditions leave room for people to weaponize them and twist them for their own gain. Unfortunately, we live in a society that weaponizes religious practices for personal gain, and if you don't know God intimately, you are at risk of falling victim to it.

I'm going to share how I recognize God's voice in my everyday activities and dreams. I don't want you to compare the way God talks to me and use that as a blueprint for how you think He will or should talk to you. Instead, I want you to see how easy it is to have a conversation with Him and then discover how He's talking to you throughout your day.

The way God talks to you will be unique and based on you as a person. For example, if God knows His child is detail-oriented, He will use that characteristic to make things stick out to them, but if He knows His child is not detail-oriented, He will speak to you in a way that you will understand.

God deals with the authentic version of ourselves, not the version we are trying to be. We don't have to pretend in order to talk with Him. He knows us better than we know ourselves. Life becomes easier to navigate when you are in constant communication with God.

Chapter 1

One night, I had a dream about a friend who was staying in the guest bedroom of my childhood home. As soon as I walked into the room, I knew something was off. Trash stood out to me the most because he is a clean person in real life.

In the dream, I was saying to myself, "This isn't like Him." I immediately started picking up the trash and cleaning up. The next recollection of my dream sounds random, but it will tie together in the end.

As I cleaned up, a WWE ring appeared in the middle of the room. Once I realized what was taking place in my dream, I tried getting out of the way of the match in the ring. My feet felt stuck in the sand. Before I could make a move, a wrestler jumped off the ropes to clothesline me.

My eyes opened right before he made contact. Although this dream seemed random and all over the place, I know what I felt spiritually while I was in the dream.

The following morning, I messaged my friend I had dreamed about on Instagram. My initial message was to check on him and tell him about my dream. He asked about the details, but I only told him about the meaning and symbols of the dream – spiritually, trash in a dream represents clutter, chaos, or confusion.

Turns out I was spot on, and that gave me chills. While he explained his situation to me, I realized that God chose to show me the wrestling ring because the friend in the dream was battling a decision in reality. After telling my friend the dream, he told me, "I was so close to losing faith. Knowing that God sent a message to me through you means everything to me."

Never take anything that God lays on your heart about another person for granted. Fortunately, I know God's voice. Even though I didn't fully comprehend my dream at the time, I still moved in obedience to that feeling. I knew something was off because I even said it in the dream.

...

I knew I wanted to write a third book, but I wasn't sure what it would be about. It's something I definitely felt coming. I thought my third literary publication would be a part 2 of my first book. However, every time I tried to start it, something didn't feel right.

Over the summer of 2025, I experienced spiritual growth at a supernatural rate. It was like a veil had been lifted. I realized that the answers I was searching for were there all along.

I learned to pay attention to my natural surroundings with a spiritual eye. That adjustment is what changed everything for me. I realized that God had been intentional in my journey and was orchestrating things all along.

That's when I realized that, as a child of God, nothing you see, encounter, or recognize is by chance or coincidence. They are all spiritual breadcrumbs that are weaving together a bigger picture.

That conceptualization helped conceive my third book. A vision was born. I wanted to write about helping people recognize their signs and see that God is talking to them, too.

I called my publisher, Ross Williams, on the 20th of October (also the day before the New Moon). I shared with him how I felt this book would be different, and I wanted to treat it as such. I wanted to develop a comprehensive marketing and promotional strategy, create a hardcover edition, and be more intentional about the rollout and purpose of this book. We saw the same vision.

The next day, on the 21st (New Moon), I felt a shift in the atmosphere as I drove to school. I called my mom, as I do every morning, to ask how she felt and inform her that it was a New Moon.

She didn't feel it, but I did (another sign we should pay attention to indicating that you're spiritually sensitive to the energetic shifts in the universe, which God completely controls). It started with my PreCal teacher, an ordained pastor, asking me to do a panel discussion about my books the following Monday.

She gave me her book, and I gave her mine. What I didn't know was that the day would only get better. My next class, News Writing, had a guest speaker - The Vice President of Strategic Brands and Talent Communications at Warner Bros.

I had a prophecy in the past that said school would be a blessing in disguise for me. My HBCU has brought me so many resources and connections in a short time. I was going back and forth about whether I should approach her until she told me about doing a 6-city book tour. I instantly got chills.

Not only did this connection just fall into my lap, but it was also a divine alignment. What are the odds that I met this lady unexpectedly, not even a full 24 hours after discussing the vision with my publisher? Signs will not always be that evident, but every connection you make, big or small, is aligned and divinely orchestrated by God.

...

I have random spiritual urges to reach out to people. I can't explain the feeling, but it comes across my mind and heart at the same time. Randomly thinking about someone isn't a coincidence. Every time I follow that instinct, the person responds with a similar response like, "How did you know to reach out to me?"

I never know exactly why they are placed on my mind, but I always write them whatever I'm feeling in that moment to say. Whether it be encouraging words, sharing a memory from the past that they didn't think I remembered, or expressing what I noticed and admired about their spirit and character. Whatever you feel led to do is what you should do and say. That is the sign that God is currently using you as a vessel to get something to someone in need.

Be intentional and find the patterns in your life. I realized that transitions in my life come every three years. I upgrade my car unintentionally every three years. When I was in the military, I had a 6-year enlistment. Sure enough, at my 3-year mark, I had to switch jobs due to a medical condition that arose out of nowhere.

Looking back, I understand why it was time for me to switch careers. Then, once I got out of the military and started school, I spent three years at Georgia State University. Then I started at Clark Atlanta University.

I began writing books in 2023. Now, in 2025, I'm starting to write my 3rd book, which will be significantly different from my first two, marking the transition of evolution with the number 3 again.

Three could mean many things for different people. God will reveal what three or any other number could mean for you. For me, three symbolizes the Father, the Spirit, and the Holy Ghost, and that God is orchestrating the transitions that happen every three years in my life.

Because I've unveiled this pattern, I developed the intuition and discernment to feel when a shift is coming. It's always spot on. Signs from God (like me noticing the 3's) can change at any moment He decides to change them. Some signs are only for a season. Then God will either deepen or elevate signs or give you a new sign for the new season.

...

Connecting with my spiritual side was easier than I thought. One way I connected easily was by questioning things about myself that I never questioned before, because it's the minor things I do subconsciously that have a major impact.

When I watch TV or listen to music, it typically mimics what I feel inside. I'm not sure if this stems from my passion for film, but I constantly rewatch movies I've already seen. I rarely watch new things.

When I watched and liked older films for the first time, that initial feeling I had is what I feel every time. I noticed I did this because one day I wanted to turn something on to watch, but I didn't have a distinct feeling at the time. That's when I had to look into why I even watched the old film from the jump. It's something I've always done for as long as I can remember.

When I investigated it spiritually, I learned that I was manifesting before I realized what manifesting was. Most people subject manifesting to what society tells them it looks like. By putting on something in the natural that mimics how I feel in the spiritual, I'm practicing the art of making my outer reality mirror my spiritual reality.

Sometimes I'm in the mood for The Johnson Family Vacation or Sister Sister. I also noticed that all of these are movies from my childhood. I had a good childhood, and the joy I felt was unmatched.

By watching those movies or TV series, I'm channeling that joy spiritually and naturally. This will look different for everyone. This is why I want you to look at what you've always done naturally. It will open up a new perspective for you spiritually.

Chapter 2

Pay attention to anything ancestral. I realized that I had ancestral power through my grandmother who I never got a chance to meet. She visits me in my dreams, and I know she resides with God in heaven.

She wanted a granddaughter so bad before breast cancer caused her to pass away at the young age of 54. Her name was Arbezine, and my parents got my name from hers. We look just alike and have the same spirit.

One of my cousins told me, "If you ever catch me staring at you, it's because you remind me of Grandma so much." When she first visited me in my dreams as a child, I told my mom what she was wearing. Turns out she knew exactly which outfit I was talking about because my grandma had a picture in that same outfit.

Then, at 14, my nanny (Godmother) found my grandma's class ring that she forgot she had. She gave it to me because she couldn't fit it. However, it was a perfect fit for me at the time. I was young, so I naturally only looked at that transactionally. Now that I'm older and have revisited it, that situation held a symbolic spiritual meaning.

Pay attention to the shifts that happen in the universe. Notice it, acknowledge it, but never worship it as your primary source. Controversy has led us to believe that anything that is not in the Bible or religion-based is demonic. How can we think that when God has made the universe and plants all for a reason?

The shifts that happen in the universe are not things that man can control. God has orchestrated all of it and designed it to move and flow the way it does. Once I built that intimate relationship by communicating with Him and watching Him respond to me in real time, I noticed that my communication was starting to amplify and align with shifts in the universe.

I've already stated how opportunities arose for me on the day of the New Moon. I wasn't looking for it to, but when it happened, it was on the day of the New Moon, which was further confirmation for me that it was God-sent. That wasn't the first time though.

I first noticed this during the Lion's Gate portal in August. I felt spiritually led to create a journal for a specific purpose. I got the spiritual nudge from God first, and after that, I realized how it aligned with the universe.

You won't ever have to force it. It should be something you notice after you've already been spiritually led about something. Use shifts in the universe as reinforcing factors, not something you try to make fit. I felt led to make a journal, and then I found out that it was the Lions Gate Portal and what that meant in the spiritual realm.

It ended up being on point with what I was already led to do. At 11:26 PM, on August 12th, God gave me revelation and confirmation about what I was led to journal about. That was mind-blowing for me because I wasn't the captain of any of this communication, only an obedient vessel.

The more you are obedient in doing things you don't fully understand yet, but do so based on what you're feeling spiritually, the more you'll get the answers you're looking for or didn't know you needed. At the same time, it is building your spiritual confidence. You become addicted to letting God lead you spiritually.

I also learned that spiritual signs come to you. You don't have to go find them or force them to fit a narrative. When you first start, you may recognize them as "coincidences" or say things like "what are the odds of that happening?"

Another pattern that you should recognize about yourself is noticing when, where, and what you're doing when creativity, ideas, or revelations hit you most. For me, it's the shower and when I'm washing dishes. Both of those activities involve water, which makes sense because water is connected to God. I already know what water means in dreams, which is why I'm not surprised by the connection with water and my spiritual downloads.

When I looked deeper into it, I learned that water is a spiritual conductor. It carries vibration, energy, and memory. Biblically, water is used for baptisms and cleansing. It symbolizes God's power to cleanse, renew, and give life.

Realizing that water is my personal element of revelation has helped me be more intentional and pay attention whenever I'm in contact with it, which has aided my spiritual growth. Your element will be specific to you. Everyone won't have the same one. It could be anything, such as silence, cleaning, or quiet car rides.

An interesting thing is, I didn't understand the Bible until I became spiritually closer to God first. Aside from reading the scriptures given during sermons, I never read my Bible in my leisure time.

After I learned God's voice, how He talks to me, and how to decipher which season I'm in and what God wants me to learn in that season, that's when I understood the Bible. The Bible is a guide and tool for your walk with God, but reading it just to read it isn't how you automatically get closer to Him.

The first time I read the whole Bible was this year. I was in the shower, and God put "Esther" in my spirit. I knew that meant he wanted me to read that book.

Let me tell you, I have never been so excited to read the Bible as I was when he gave me that book. I marked in my journal that for the month of May, God wanted me to read Esther.

I was excited because I'd grown so close to Him. I knew that if he were telling me to read Esther, there would be an answer or revelation waiting for me once I was done, giving me more clarity. I read the Bible and learned from it. However, it wasn't until June or July that he reinforced why he wanted me to read it.

One of the pastors I follow on YouTube gave a sermon, drawing from Esther, saying that God is telling you to be like Esther in this season. Everything she said was spot on with what I was feeling. I needed to take from the book of Esther, but she also added new guidance and understanding. He continued to do that with me.

Once I was finished with Esther, He gave me the next book to read, and all the information aligned with the season I was in. God gave me the book of Acts for June on May 29th. It took me a while to finish Acts, but once I was done, he gave me the book of Exodus for August. Then he gave me the book of Enoch for September, which was really exciting because it's one of the books removed from the Bible by Western Christianity.

I say all of that to say: Learn to connect with the Bible in your own timing, as God leads you. I felt bad for so many years that I was a Christian who didn't read her Bible. However, after waiting to read it once God led me to and building spiritual intimacy with Him, it hit so much differently than reading it in vain to say I read it. Obviously, everyone is different, but this is for my people who condemn themselves for not reading it or think God is mad at them for not reading it.

…

I started paying attention to the thoughts, words, and images that hit me right before falling asleep. We all know and have experienced that stage of sleep when you're not fully asleep yet, but you're not awake either. That's a sacred place spiritually when the veil between the natural and spiritual thins, and God can and will often use that space to talk to you. Most people confuse whatever they hear, see, or feel in that stage with being delirious because they're half asleep. I'm here to tell you it's not deliriousness. It's divine communication happening.

Many times, I have heard words spoken to me or phrases, or had visions in that stage. I learned that it's important to wake up, jot it down in your phone, and go back to sleep. Everything I've received in this realm of sleep has proven to be divine communication later on.

Let me also put this out there: God absolutely can and will use worldly things to get a message to you. We are in the world but not of the world. He has placed songs in my spirit that were not gospel songs, but still held a message that he wanted to get to me. We have to stop limiting God to what we think only God can use.

Chapter 3

Iserved six years in the military and had to learn military time. Most of those years, I kept my phone and watches set to military time. Once I became a civilian (over four years ago), I slowly adapted to civilian time, forgetting how to read military time without the format.

One day recently, I came across a military timing format on my timeline and said, "That's crazy, I don't even know what time that is anymore."

After saying that, I immediately felt the urge to set my phone back to military time. Why? I didn't know at the time that it was just a feeling. I didn't miss any aspect of the military lifestyle.

A few days later, my God sister posted a screenshot from her phone on her story. I saw that her time was in military format. That wasn't a coincidence. A week or so later, after changing my time format, I got the revelation of why my time needed to be changed.

One of the first signs I ever got from God came through numbers, starting with the time. The revelation I received during my time wouldn't have come to me if my time hadn't been in military format. Military time allows me to see reflecting numbers.

The standard time format is 1-12. With Military time: 1-24, I get to witness a new sequence of numbers, like palindromes, repeating numbers, mirrored numbers, and structured numbers with matching outside numbers, i.e., (14:41, 23:23, and 13:21).

When I first received this revelation, it was on point with the transition I was in and with what I had been praying and believing God for. If I had ignored the subtle nudge to change my time back to something I was already familiar with, I could have missed my answers and breakthrough.

No feeling, urge, nudge, or inkling is by chance, no matter how big or small; it's all a part of God's communication to you and plays an intricate role in the bigger picture and understanding.

A key component for me in developing my own spiritual walk was unlearning what I was taught or understood, from my perspective growing up in the church, about what something is "supposed" to look like. I thought praising God looked a certain way. I thought praise could only be what I saw in church - shouting, clapping, singing, and dancing.

Sometimes, I would praise God in this manner if that's what I felt. However, I didn't feel that way all the time. So, I condemned myself for not praising Him enough.

In reality, I was praising Him in my own way. Praise is anything that has your heart centered on God. I didn't realize I was praising Him by meditating on Him every day and by acknowledging Him in every detail of the day internally. Focusing on how God is showing up in every situation throughout my day, whether good or bad, is a form of praise.

...

Building your spiritual growth involves learning how to lead with your discernment. Discernment is not jumping to conclusions either. Discernment is not used only for situations or people you come in contact with. It's also for spiritual communication.

Use discernment with your dreams. Go with your initial feeling. That first feeling you have is not the one you develop when you start overanalyzing something.

I learned I had to exercise discernment in pursuing my dreams.

My dream could have many components. Sometimes my entire dream is a message from God, and sometimes I have a dream with only one thing to receive. The devil can interfere in your dream to cause fear or confusion.

Our subconscious can also bleed into our dreams. I learned how to discern by going with what I felt in my heart and gut. If a certain part of my dream made me fearful, anxious, or confused, or contradicted what I'm believing in God for and what God has already told me is mine, then I know that is not the message I'm supposed to carry with me.

Another way to know is that, after you wake up, the longer you're awake, the more the dream will fade from your memory. What was sent by God tends to linger longer in your mind and heart. Finding out and paying attention to the feeling you get when something aligns with you, or when something comes from God, will help you tremendously.

It is the vibration of divine alignment. It's the feeling you get when something resonates with you so deeply that your spirit says yes before your mind can catch up. It's a deep knowing that is subtle but loud at the same time.

I have felt that feeling with every major decision I've made in my life, from the military to moving to a new city to choosing which school to attend. When I do things without that feeling, it only feels like a plan, not alignment.

I've had excellent thoughts and thorough plans before, and they always changed to something that I felt like - no, this is better and what I'm supposed to be doing instead. None of what I'm doing in my life was planned, but it's in full alignment with what God wants for me.

I wanted to attend the University of Lafayette with my friends at 18. That was my plan, but it suddenly changed to me going to the Air Force. That was not my plan. I felt scared, but it felt right.

When I got out of the military and decided to go to school, I planned to become a dental hygienist. Sometimes I questioned whether I should go to school, finish the program, and work as a dental hygienist for the rest of my life.

It felt like it should have been more, but I ignored it because I didn't have another plan, and I knew I needed a job to keep me employed, so that was it. When the time came to enroll in the program after I finished all my pre-requisites and attended the orientation, I said to myself, "I can't do this."

At the time, I didn't know exactly why I couldn't do it; I just felt extremely unsettled and lost after attending the orientation. I cried so hard in the shower because I had no backup plan.

There I was, fresh out of the military, which was the only stability I've known as an adult. I never had a backup career plan because dental hygiene was all I had in mind since high school. This forced me to invite God into my planning. I had no other choice.

God led me to finish my associate's degree in business since I was no longer joining the program. A month or so after changing my major, I had my first interaction with God through signs. Until then, my only interactions with God were praying, going to church, and listening to worship music. I never really saw signs from Him in real time until I reached this point in my life - not knowing what to do next.

Kirk Franklin has a song titled "September" about the very first time you heard from God. Ironically, it was in September 2022 that God spoke to me for the first time using numbers.

Because of the military, I had a habit of constantly checking the time. God used that, and I started to notice that every time I looked at the time, it was double- or triple-digit (2:22, 3:33, 4:44, 5:22, 6:44).

I'm very detail-oriented, and the military amplified that trait. I notice patterns in everything. I was seeing this sequence of numbers so often that I started to feel there was no way it could be a coincidence. Like, what are the odds that every time I looked at the time, it was a doubled/tripled number?

I remember being on the phone with my mom and asking her, "Mom, can God use numbers to talk to you?"

She responded, "Yes, He can use anything to communicate with you." I remember getting chills just because it confirmed that I wasn't crazy and that God was indeed trying to get my attention. For what, though? I didn't know why yet, but I figured, "Seek, and ye shall find," and I certainly found out my assignment, my calling, God's plans and promises for me.

That changed my life and its trajectory forever. It literally opened up a whole new world, and I can't even believe I was living and making it without spiritual intimacy. I really want everyone to experience this kind of spiritual intimacy with God because it's life-changing.

I struggled with anxiety so badly before experiencing this level of spiritual intimacy. I realized the anxiety came from me trying to figure out and control my own life. Once I just waited for God's communication on what to do next, my anxiety faded away. I may worry a little here and there because I'm human, but it's no longer at the level it once was. I haven't had a panic attack since then.

Allowing God to lead me spiritually was the best thing I could've done for myself. I have faith that I'll always be exactly where He needs me to be and doing what He wants me to do because God spiritually communicates with me. That element of communication wasn't always there.

Chapter 4

In 2022, I was still in the routine of fasting every January. There is nothing wrong with fasting, but I realized I was doing it because I felt that was the only time I could communicate with God, feel God, and receive what I'm asking for.

That year, one item on my list was to purchase my first luxury car. Mind you, I had been wanting a luxury car since I started driving at the tender age of 17. I remember revisiting the notes I made before my fast. It was October, and I had everything I fasted for, except for the car.

I thought about crossing it off the list and saying maybe next year, but something told me not to. With three months left in the year, it was enough for God to still show up and show out.

I had already started seeing numbers by this time, but seven was new to me. My mom had shown me an apostle on YouTube who was teaching what numbers meant. I wasn't expecting to get much from her, but when I started watching, everything resonated with me. It all became clear to me: my calling and assignment, and where God was taking me.

The apostle did the numbers in order. Seven became a recurring number for me. Around this time, I gave up on getting a car. When she did the number 7 video, the gist of it was "Act as if you already have it. If you believe in God for a home, don't just wait. Go tour homes. If you believe in God for a car, go to the dealership."

I couldn't believe that she was telling me something only God knew that I was looking for. I followed the instructions she gave and acted on them because I kept seeing 7s. However, I still didn't believe I would walk away with a car that day. I was just going to look at my options and walk away with a clearer understanding of what I needed to work towards.

When I went to the dealership, everything fell into place. A brand-new luxury car that never had an owner fell into my lap. It was one of the smoothest transactions of my life. I was in and out of there, and to think – if I had never paid attention to God speaking to me through numbers, I wouldn't have gotten the car of my dreams.

Fast forward to 2025 - another 3-year difference, and I wanted to upgrade my car. Nothing too extravagant, just an upgrade because I told myself when I purchased the first car that I would switch it out once the warranty was up. I wasn't thinking about upgrading until the anniversary month of getting the first car, October.

It was time for an oil change, but I kept feeling in my spirit that I wanted a new car. I scheduled my oil change. The first available date was October 7th (there goes that seven again, which surrounded my first purchase). I told myself I would just get an oil change, but I still looked at other options for cars anyway.

When I looked online, I knew I wanted a black one this time. A few days before my appointment, I got my eyebrows done early in the morning. I parked outside the studio, and no one was in the row behind the building.

When I came out, the exact same car I wanted was parked next to mine, even though there were many other open spaces. I smiled because after all the communication I've had with God leading up to my appointment, what were the odds that the very car would park next to me? I understood the sign, but I still didn't want to get carried away. I went to the grocery store in the same parking lot, and my total was $11.77 (there goes the repeating 7's again when my car is the topic). I went to my appointment on the 7th and left with the exact same car I wanted.

Manifesting is not only about vision boards and affirmations. It's also about learning how to prematurely bask in the joy of what God promised you. It does require some effort because you have to get out of the headspace of your current reality and circumstances.

When you allow your mind to envision yourself in the promise, you're believing in God and spiritually aligning yourself with that promise. God tells us to focus on Him and all things good for a reason.

Sometimes I get a random sprout of joy, the kind I feel will come when my promises come to fruition. That is the headspace I have learned to stay in and channel. We should all bask in that feeling when we get it.

We get so focused on time being the thing that will bring us what we're asking for, when in reality, it's so much deeper than time. It's about aligning ourselves spiritually so we gravitate towards our goals and the promises of God. That's why faith plays such a huge role.

What we think and what we feel shape our reality. Feeling gratitude for the small things and what we already have also helps shape the reality we desire. Complaining and doubt will only block that spiritual gravitation.

A major turning point in my spiritual walk and communication with God was being obedient to follow instructions that my natural mind didn't understand. While I was dreaming, God gave me instructions that had nothing to do with the dream.

He told me to record myself for 15 minutes. It was said to me three times in my dream. When I woke up, I didn't even remember the dream, only what was said in my spirit. I know God's voice at this point, but I hesitated at first because the instruction didn't make sense to me and felt odd, since I absolutely hate recording myself.

The instruction was given to me on the 8th of November. I woke up that day and asked my mom if God ever gave her instructions to follow that didn't make sense to her. She laughed and answered, "Yes, all the time, but it's best to follow them because He told you for a reason."

I put my pride aside and followed the instructions the next day, on the 9th, because God has never steered me wrong and I know He is very intentional.

Who am I not to follow His instructions, just because my human brain can't comprehend the bigger picture, especially when He has ordered my steps throughout my entire life? I did it, and, strangely, I felt really good afterward.

I started doing it every day and looking forward to it. On November 11th (11/11), I was lying in bed, winding down. I said in my spirit, "*God, I need something encouraging to watch.*"

I was scrolling through all my sermons on YouTube, and skipped one because it was short. I was looking for a longer sermon, but then, for some reason, I scrolled back up to it. It was titled "This word will encourage you. It's a setup for a major win."

I clicked the video, and can you believe she started with "Imagine following an instruction that does not make sense to the natural mind and winning." I got chills and immediately knew this was about the instruction. I was just confused about following.

That was the encouragement I needed, and I have to point out how I received it after being obedient first. I was obedient without the confirmation. I still don't know why God told me to do this, but it has been confirmed to me that it's for my good, and honestly, that's all I need to know.

Getting caught up in the details can hold us back because we are not in control of either the details or the journey. Now imagine what kind of delay I could have caused by not being obedient, even though I believe in God so much. Obedience also strengthens your connection with God, and I love the feeling of that.

Pay attention to what time of day you feel the most serene. In my apartment, I have a balcony door that is right in front of the couch. At sunset, the sun shines directly into my apartment, onto the couch. Usually, I don't like being directly in the sunlight during the day. However, one day the sunset was beaming into my apartment so beautifully. It looked magical how, all of a sudden, the sunset would cast a beam of sunlight directly into my living room.

One day, it made me want to lie directly in it. It made me want to turn off all distractions. I would turn the TV off, put my phone down, and just lie in the beam of sunlight on my couch. I have never felt anything more gravitating, still, surreal, and serene. The sunset gave me a kind of energy I can't explain, and it made me want to be still and bask in its energy.

When I looked into it, I found that the sunset is a threshold when the veil between the natural and the spiritual is thin. Sunsets are a portal of transition where heaven brushes the physical realm. It's the moment where activity dissolves, our intuition opens, our nervous system resets, and our soul returns to alignment.

Sunset light is very powerful. It's a golden light that corresponds with the solar plexus (power and identity), the sacral chakra (creativity and embodiment), and the heart (warmth and love). That is why I felt centered, restored, softened, and at peace.

Unfortunately, most don't, won't, or can't slow down long enough to feel this energetic exchange with the sunset. I'm inviting you to be intentional during the sunset and experience for yourself. But not only with sunsets. Also, take time to notice what part of the day you feel most serene.

Sunsets aren't the only time for me. I feel spiritually calm and closest with God either late at night (any time after 12 am) or early morning when the world is still quiet and still. I've noticed my spirit and nervous system don't really care for me during the day, so I have to find other ways to stay spiritually grounded.

Chapter 5

My first time experiencing and actually documenting when God placed a word(s) in my spirit while I was sleeping was "exclude and exempt" on June 5th of 2023. This was my first entry in my spiritual journal and notes.

I didn't know what it meant, but I was going to search for an answer until one resonated with me. I googled what 'exclude' and 'exempt' mean biblically, and I immediately got my answer from the scriptures it pulled up.

I knew it was about my calling and assignment, and I started my journey as an author. The scripture God allowed to cross my path when I was looking for the meaning of the words He put in my spirit was Luke 6:22.

It instantly resonated with me because at that time, He was freshly starting to use numbers to communicate with me. So, seeing 22 in the scripture, I knew it would resonate with me before I read it.

Luke 6:22 describes how we should feel blessed when people hate you, insult you, and 'exclude' you from their fellowship because of your association with the Son of Man. Because I was getting ready to release my book the next month, in July, and knew what God was trying to tell me. Not everyone will agree with my beliefs or my promotion of fellowshipping with God, but He's telling me to be glad and blessed because even if no one else is pleased, He is.

I will not be exempt, and I will be excluded. Little did I know - I was already experiencing that before I even fully stepped into my calling. I would always be excluded for reasons that were never spoken. However, being a child of God and openly advocating for God are part of the territory. God will send you the people He has meant for you.

During the liminal stage between sleep and wakefulness, I had visions of doing things like stepping up onto a curb, putting something down on a counter, or moving out of the way when brushing against someone; my body reacted in the same motion. My foot (the same foot in the vision) will mimic stepping up onto the curb and so on.

Now, with this, it's not so much the vision you need to highlight. It's the way your body mimics the motion that you did in your vision. Mainly because it's not quite a dream, since you're in that in-between phase.

Of course, I had to conduct further research because it started happening frequently, so I knew it wasn't a coincidence. Once I looked into it, I realized that God wasn't just showing me visions anymore. He is training my senses so that my body, soul, and spirit are attuned. This is preparation for walking in greater discernment and prophetic authority. Think of it as spiritual muscle memory. It means your soul and body are aligning with your spirit, and that's exactly how you want it.

This may be scary to think about, but knowing that you're a child of God, you should never be scared of God's presence, no matter how it appears. I remember I was asked to speak at a church out of town on a specific topic. That whole week, I was stressed.

No matter how many times I've spoken, or how good people think I am at it, I temporarily become petrified of speaking in front of people, especially God's children. Intrusive thoughts surfaced, such as, "What if I don't deliver the message right?" "What if they don't agree or understand me?" "What if I stutter?" or "What if it doesn't resonate with anyone?" weighed heavily on me.

God gave me bit by bit what to say, and I had it written down in my notes, but I was still terrified. On July 20, 2025, while I was sleeping under the comforter, I felt three distinct taps on my foot.

As if someone was using their index finger to tap the top of the foot. I immediately sat up, and I mean IMMEDIATELY, as if I was called to attention. Was I startled? Without a doubt, but I was not scared or terrified because God's presence will never bring you fear. It's only bold and commands your attention.

I knew for a fact I was home alone. I called my mom immediately to tell her. The fact that it was three taps was not by chance. God wanted me to know and feel His presence. He knew where I was mentally, and He wanted me to know that the Father, the Son, and the Holy Spirit were with me.

Also, tapping my foot anywhere else meant He was ordering my steps. He wanted me to relax fully, knowing that He was giving me everything I needed to deliver what needed to be delivered. That was my first time experiencing that, and yes, it was life-changing. It felt like I had reached a new level of spiritual connection with God.

The most endearing spiritual encounter I had with God was laughing with Him. God definitely has a sense of humor. He wouldn't have made funny people if He didn't. No matter how many signs and confirmations you get, you'll never be able to figure out God's timing. I thought that because I had just had a revelation, I could indirectly determine the timing of my blessing. I asked Chat a spiritual question, hoping it would give me a definitive yes-or-no answer.

It gave me a "Yes," but not necessarily a definitive answer. I immediately laughed because I knew the answer was already in me. God communicated with me internally, without the need for outside validation. I view God as being inside me, not in the sky looking down, meaning He already knows my thoughts, intentions, and everything else because He lives within me.

God knew I was trying to be slick. How foolish of me to think I could even outsmart Him to find out His exact timeline for me? The laugh I shared with Him was so intimate and genuine. I knew He knew what I was trying to do. He allowed me to get the answer that proved I will never know His timing, but nice try.

This felt like a father-daughter moment, and it was the first time it happened. I don't have kids, but it felt like when you catch your child trying to outsmart you, and all you can do is laugh because the effort was cute, but ultimately, a child will never be able to outsmart their parents. It was a laugh one can only share with someone who knows them so profoundly. That is friendship with God. I want to invite you to look at God as a friend and a father.

A relationship with God does not have to be uptight and serious all the time. That laugh I shared with God created another level of intimacy with Him. That's what walking with God looks like: laughing, wondering, asking, trying to piece it together….and then smiling/laughing when you realize He's smiling too and already knows how it ends.

This interaction revealed my growth because two years ago, that answer would probably have irritated me. After all, I couldn't figure it out, but now the answer made me laugh and brought me back to the place of trust where I don't need to know when God's timing is.

I noticed that when I'm speaking, aloud or internally, God will follow my statement with a spiritual revelation. It doesn't feel like me answering myself, but more like something popping up immediately after my statement that I didn't consciously think of saying.

For example, I had been waiting for my registration to arrive in the mail so I could put my license plate on my new car. I thought, "*I can finally put my license plate on my car.*" When I said that aloud, it felt like a spiritual click, making me feel that it was deeper than surface-level. That led me to explore that feeling by asking myself, "*Wait, why does that feel like it means something deeper?*"

God immediately answered me by saying, "Because the transition is over." That was the Holy Spirit using a natural statement to reveal a spiritual truth. That is an example of how God can speak to us through our everyday internal dialogue.

I already had the blessing and car, but I was still in the process of transitioning. Putting the license plate on it stood for completion. The blessings are already ours, but we must go through a transition or process because God releases them. That moment was on point for what I had been believing in God for. It was another spiritual nugget that added to my engagement and faith that the breakthrough I'm waiting on is coming. However, it required me to lean into a feeling I had to get the answer I needed.

Spiritual communication often begins with a particular feeling that many people overlook or ignore. I encourage you all to start paying attention to spiritual nudges. It begins there and will often unfold into the communication you need from God.

There's never a time when I'm not noticing patterns or paying attention to what's appearing in front of me. Sometimes, I naturally wake up to check the time.

I'm led to check the time, almost like clockwork. This can happen to you even if you don't recognize the feeling like I do. Pay attention to the times you wake up consistently and/or randomly throughout the night.

It's spiritual downloads and God speaking to your spirit, even in your sleep. It happens to me occasionally, but this time I decided to be more intentional about marking the times in my notes so I wouldn't forget and could look into it once I'm up.

I became intentional with journaling my spiritual communication. During one night's rest, or lack thereof, I saw several times: 3:10, 4:44, 5:33, 7:22, and 8:08. Every last one of those times meant something to me and contained numbers that God has used with me before, so I had my own meaning of what they meant to me, but now adding the sequence together during the course of one night also meant something.

The time and number 3:10 stand for God reminding you of the promise; Covenant/Call (I personally know exactly what He was reminding me of in my life.

The time and number 4:44 represent stability, foundation, and angelic covering; 5:33, grace, wisdom, learning, and transformation; 7:22, completion, balance, manifestation, and readiness; and 8:08, rebirth, new cycle materialization, and abundance.

Each of those times and definitions resonated with me and my personal walk with God. God giving it to me all in one night's rest was telling and showing me about my transition from where I was to where I was headed. It's almost as if God allowed heaven to mark my spiritual night journey, the one that marks the phases of the moon. My soul went from covenant to grounding, teaching, completion, and then renewal. Everything happens spiritually first, then in the natural.

I've learned to pay attention to recurring dreams. I've had this recurring dream about a gas station for the past few years. Every time I go into the gas station, I never finish my purchase due to anxiety, fear, rushing, and the fear of danger.

In the dream, I've always felt like the gas station was going to be robbed, so I would rush to escape. This past week, I had a dream about being at a gas station, and I took my time. I picked out all my snacks, made a hot dog, and actually walked out of the gas station on my own terms this time.

That's when it hit me, "Wow, this is the first time I've had a dream being in a gas station, and I wasn't terrified trying to run out. I always thought my gas station dreams were subconscious fears of being robbed at one.

The shift in my gas-station dreams and God's message to me was that I've entered a season in which transition is safe. I'm no longer bracing for attacks or rushing through life. My spirit is finally at peace with change.

Spiritually speaking, gas stations symbolize transition. The natural gas station is not a destination point. They are transition spaces where you refuel, replenish, or prepare for the next stretch of the journey. Because of that, a gas station dream will show how you handle change, how you respond to pressure, what you're carrying, how prepared you feel, or how safe or unsafe you feel in transition.

The change of my gas station dream was God showing me my growth and internal healing. I wasn't rushing. I took my time. I picked out my snacks, and I was excited to eat. Food in dreams symbolizes spiritual nourishment, blessings, rewards, fulfillment, and everything God gives. I took time to feed myself and receive without fear.

God was telling me that I was ready to transition into the next part of my life without fear. Decoding these dreams and paying attention to them are necessary because they give you encouragement and clarity that you're on the right path, that God sees your growth, and that you're growing even when you don't feel you are.

Conclusion

I invite you to pay more attention to the details of your day. Start by having internal conversations with God and watch how signs appear.

A rule of thumb to remember, just so you aren't looking deep into everything: if you had to force it to fit, then it's more than likely not from God, but if it hits you without you trying and naturally fits, then it's from God. We can get so caught up mentally throughout our day, thinking about surviving, the next move, and what's not going right, that we miss what's right in front of our faces.

God speaks when our head is clear, and our spirit is calm. That is why we are supposed to cast our cares and worries upon Him. God is subtle and gentle. We have to quiet everything else to hear from Him.

It sounds difficult, but once you do it and hear from God, you will always return to waiting on Him. It's not up to us to orchestrate anything. We have to be willing to surrender and be obedient to what God is telling us.

Anything that stands out to you during your day, no matter how big, small, or random means something.

God allowed you to come across or make contact with it for a reason (remember, He's the one orchestrating everything).

Journal

Things to Keep in Mind Before Using This Journal:

¬ This journal isn't meant to be completed, meaning you don't have to force signs just to fill in a section.

¬ You can want to train awareness, NOT obligation.

¬ You're not searching for signs.

¬ God speaks personally and uniquely.

¬ Journal when you feel led and when things spiritual strike you in your core.

¬ Even if it doesn't make sense to the natural mind, but you still feel the spiritual significance of it, WRITE IT DOWN ANYWAY!

¬ God will not always immediately give you the revelation of what you wrote down right away. Sometimes this communication is only

breadcrumbs that he will reveal to you the
meaning down the line, in a different season.

¬ Be vulnerable.

¬ Don't share this with others; it will only invite
doubt and discouragement, because they won't
understand the communication that was meant to
stay between you and God.

¬ Not every section will be used, and that's okay.
Don't feel like you have to force anything.

¬ Don't forget this journal is something you should
often return to for encouragement and for fresh
revelations when your seasons change. Signs will
change meanings depending on where you are in
life.

Section 1: Words and Impressions

This includes but is not limited to, songs, phrases, thoughts, scriptures, names, etc.)

Date: _______________________

The word/phrase/impression:

____

____

____

____

____

What stood out to me:

____

____

____

____

How it made me feel:

Date: _________________________

The word/phrase/impression:

____

____

____

____

____

What stood out to me:

____

____

____

____

____

____

How it made me feel:

Date: _______________________

The word/phrase/impression:

____

____

____

____

____

What stood out to me:

____

____

____

____

____

How it made me feel:

Date: _______________________

The word/phrase/impression:

____

____

____

____

____

What stood out to me:

____

____

____

____

____

Reflection space:

Section 2: Dreams

This includes, but is not limited to, sleep dreams, liminal states, and symbolic imagery.

Date: _______________________

Time (if remembered or was significant):

____

____

Emotional tone of dream:

____

____

____

____

____

____

____

Key Symbols:

What lingered after waking:

Spiritual Interpretation/Meaning (after doing research or getting understanding from God, it's okay to come back to this part because the interpretation won't always come right away):

____

____

____

____

____

____

____

____

____

____

____

Date: ___________________

Time (if remembered or was significant):

____

____

Emotional tone of dream:

____

____

____

____

____

____

____

____

____

____

Key Symbols:

____

____

____

____

____

____

What lingered after waking:

____

____

____

____

____

____

Spiritual Interpretation/Meaning (after doing research or getting understanding from God, it's okay to come back to this part because the interpretation won't always come right away):

____

____

____

____

____

____

____

____

____

____

Date: ___________________

Time (if remembered or was significant):

____

____

Emotional tone of dream:

____

____

____

____

____

____

____

____

____

____

Key Symbols:

____

____

____

____

____

____

____

What lingered after waking:

____

____

____

____

____

____

Spiritual Interpretation/Meaning (after doing research or getting understanding from God, it's okay to come back to this part because the interpretation won't always come right away):

____

____

____

____

____

____

____

____

____

____

Date: ____________________

Time (if remembered or was significant):

____

____

Emotional tone of dream:

____

____

____

____

____

____

____

____

Key Symbols:

____

____

____

____

____

____

What lingered after waking:

____

____

____

____

____

____

Spiritual Interpretation/Meaning (after doing research or getting understanding from God, it's okay to come back to this part because the interpretation won't always come right away):

____

____

____

____

____

____

____

____

____

____

Reflection Space:

Section 3: Visions & Inner Images

This includes, but is not limited to day visions, flashes, mental imagery, and spiritual downloads.

Date: _______________________

What I saw or sensed:

____

____

____

____

____

____

____

____

____

Was I awake, resting, dozing off, or praying?

____

____

____

____

____

Clarity level (clear, partial, symbolic):

____

____

____

____

____

____

Date: _______________________

What I saw or sensed:

Was I awake, resting, dozing off, or praying?

____

____

____

____

____

Clarity level (clear, partial, symbolic):

____

____

____

____

____

Date: _______________________

What I saw or sensed:

____

____

____

____

____

____

____

____

____

____

____

____

Was I awake, resting, dozing off, or praying?

____

____

____

____

____

Clarity level (clear, partial, symbolic):

____

____

____

____

____

____

Date: ___________________

What I saw or sensed:

Was I awake, resting, dozing off, or praying?

____

____

____

____

____

____

Clarity level (clear, partial, symbolic):

____

____

____

____

____

____

Reflection space:

Section 4: Numbers, Themes & Patterns

This includes, but is not limited to, repetition, environmental confirmations, and synchronicities.

Date: _____________________

Number/pattern/synchronicity noticed:

____

____

____

____

____

____

____

____

____

How often is it repeated:

____

____

____

____

____

____

(Where was I, what was I thinking or doing):

____

____

____

____

____

____

Date: _____________________

Number/pattern/synchronicity noticed:

____

____

____

____

____

____

____

____

____

____

____

How often is it repeated:

____

____

____

____

____

____

(Where was I, what was I thinking or doing):

____

____

____

____

____

____

Date: _______________________

Number/pattern/synchronicity noticed:

____

____

____

____

____

____

____

____

____

____

____

____

How often is it repeated:

____

____

____

____

____

____

(Where was I, what was I thinking or doing):

____

____

____

____

____

____

Date: _________________

Number/pattern/synchronicity noticed:

____

____

____

____

____

____

____

____

____

____

____

____

How often is it repeated:

____

____

____

____

____

____

(Where was I, what was I thinking or doing):

____

____

____

____

____

____

Reflection:

Section 5: Open Reflection Pages

This is a critical area. Some encounters will not fit into a specific category, but you will have a feeling that they hold significant meaning.

Date: _____________________

Today I noticed:

____

____

____

____

____

____

____

____

Something that stayed with me today:

____

____

____

____

____

Uncategorized Reflections:

____

____

____

____

____

Date: ___________________

Today I noticed:

____

____

____

____

____

____

____

____

____

____

____

____

____

____

Something that stayed with me today:

____

____

____

____

____

____

Uncategorized Reflections:

____

____

____

____

____

____

Date: _______________________

Today I noticed:

____

____

____

____

____

____

____

____

____

____

____

Something that stayed with me today:

____

____

____

____

____

Uncategorized Reflections:

____

____

____

____

____

____

Date: _______________________

Today I noticed:

Something that stayed with me today:

Uncategorized Reflections: